DEVON LIBRARIES
Please return/renew this item by the due date
Renew on tel. 0345 155 1001 or at
www.devonlibraries.org.uk

Mo

12. OCT 21.

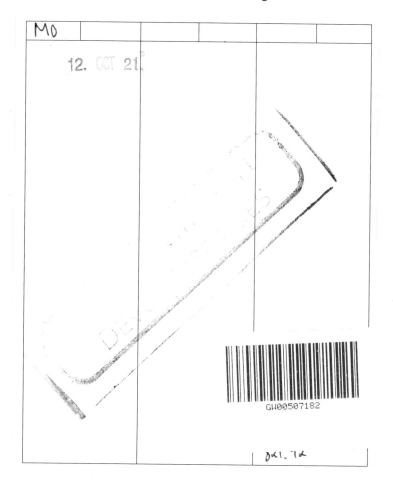

D 1. 7 d

Moor Poets

VOLUME III

A collection of contemporary poetry

Published by
MOOR POETS

First published in 2013 by Moor Poets
a Dartmoor-based writers' group, Southwest England

Moor Poets, Oak Cottage, Poundsgate,
Newton Abbot, TQ13 7NU

www.moorpoets.org.uk

Cover design is from a collagraph print:
'Wheal Betsy' by Anita Reynolds
www.anitareynolds.com

Typesetting: main text in Constantia, cover and title page in
Humana Serif Light

A CIP record of this book is available from the British Library.

Printed by:
The Printing Press, Plymouth, Devon:
www.the-printing-press.co.uk

ISBN 978-0-9551114-2-6

INTRODUCTION

Moor Poets has just passed its tenth anniversary. There can be no better way of celebrating this than by sharing our poetry. Here in our third and best anthology to date, you will find poems on subjects as diverse as cracking walnuts, a gibbet, considerations of sunspots and January. The poems in this latest anthology reflect our individual considerations of the world, our experiences, our passions and our memories.

It is always a challenge to select the best work for an anthology such as this, and then to arrange the poems in the most readable order. The selection and ordering of sixty poems for this volume, the work of thirty three Moor Poets, was a pleasure for those involved. The quality of the poems selected reflects a richness of language and inventiveness through wide variation in style.

Dartmoor is the spiritual and often the physical location of Moor Poets' creative efforts, and although many members live within the National Park boundary, others reside in the surrounding areas and beyond. Many of our events, workshops and readings take place in Dartmoor locations. But our poetry is as wide-ranging as our backgrounds and perceptions of the world. I trust you will enjoy its many different flavours.

I would like to collectively acknowledge and thank all the individuals and committed groups of our members who have generously brought their skills to this project, and who have seen it through to fruition.

Graham Burchell (Chairman, Moor Poets)

CONTENTS

THE EGG COLLECTOR

The mute swan eggs were the first, pale grey
and four inches long. He blew their life out
through two pinholes. Then the deep blue
of the American robin, he had to pay for those,
but that vividness against white tissue was
enough to sway any doubt, like the house finch
sapphire, tiny in his palm, with dots of black,
or the northern mocking bird, a delicate green
speckled brown. He catalogued and laid them
with the others, in shredded paper nests, ranged
in a stack of narrow drawers that reached halfway
to the ceiling, sliding open with ease when his hands
were tempted. He lived in his box house with
these jewels he'd decided on, nothing gold or glass;
glitter was a garbled song. He only knew one note.

Julie-Ann Rowell

CHAPEL ON THE MOOR

Beside the toppling stream
a curve of stones –
              a ruined shelter.
Next to a quiver of harebells
spreads the yellow and ochre
              of *eggs and bacon*.

He notes the piety of bumble bees
among the ling,
              the sacred characters
on the lipped petals of orchids

By day he hunts among the bogs
for definitions of stalk and flower
              noticing the fur of anthers
the sticky tentacles of sundew
the scent – only at dusk –
              of butterfly orchids

Moths flutter towards the dappled
moon of his face
              owls shepherding
the bleating stars. Rain crackles
              like incense

Year by year
his congregation settles into families of flora
              Umbelliferae, Rosaceae, Compositae
and he finds that words in his sermons
              attract bees
while his finger-ends burst into leaf and flower

Rebecca Gethin

William Keble Martin (who was the author of The Concise British Flora) and his brothers
built an open-air chapel close to Headland Warren on Dartmoor in 1904. OS SX666 666

SPRING GARDENER

Sunlight scrapes the condensation
from windows earlier each morning
and drills eyes awake.

Timpani of sparrows and finches
cacophony of crows and magpies
alarm ears awake.

Voles, shrews, young rabbits
catapulted through the catflap
invade the yawning house.

I flee into the teeming garden:
at last the fledging hawthorn hedge
flickers green for go.

I weed and hoe and plant and sow.
I flex and stretch and judder and groan
like a rusty spring.

Joan Stansbury

APPRECIATING PRIMROSE

For the breath of you
for the optimistic torch of you
for the cool cloud cream of you
for the luminous you paint on dirt-grey days

when your fine flims of convex
milk the width of twilight
under arched cotoneaster.
Shadows lift you
          and you lift the shadows.
Five hearted petals
hint at coffee, silk and coriander
and your core is earth and fire,
yellow for the peace
of being primrose.
As inquisitive as overhanging birch,
branches flecked with lichen,
          dancing in the wind
that chanced you deep between
the hard blades of hartstongue.

For the wren of you, sturdy flicker in the hedge
for your lithe signals of the Spring
for the dream-texture
thank you *Primula vulgaris*

Ian Royce Chamberlain

OUT OF HIBERNATION

All the songbirds outside in new light are awake
snapping their bright eyes open and singing
to bring on their nestlings.

But I am asleep, I say
and still in the hold of a good healing dream
full of dancing and longing and ferny shadow.

All the creatures in my brain are awake
snapping their yellow eyes open like celandines
but I am asleep, I say

and was dreaming that it was a warm day
such a thing, very close
very warm.

All the poems in my head are awake
snippety snapping like winged things
like so many sheets to the wind

driving the agitant flow in the top of my heart
but I am asleep I say and dreaming a shady wood
everything moistened by leaf life in the air

as it wraps its kindling arms around me
so I shed all my clothes for no reason
but for the feeling of being free.

Susan Taylor

SLOE GIN

The best, protected by an armoury of angry spines,
flaunt their ripeness as they bob
out over the quarry's edge and mock
with abundant fruitfulness the cold blue sky.

Wielding a needle from the sewing kit
I lance their bitterness;
deep purple dye stains finger tips
and lodges firmly underneath my nails.

Some are far too large to slip
easily down the bottle's throat,
must be rammed in, pushed, protesting,
leaking juices out.

Sugar is funnelled into half-full bottles
smothering fruit in its grainy white embrace,
and sifting, shifting into all the gaps in readiness
for a dousing with the clarity of gin.

Sealed, labelled, stored and hidden
the bottles lie almost forgotten
for many months,
abandoned to the dark

until with winter past
sunshine emerges and at last
sweetness touches the lips.
It's a slow process,

this transformation
through darkness into light,
from pain and bitterness
to sweet maturity.

Alwyn Marriage

NOISY COUPLETS FROM THE 'CRUMBS AND CUPPA', SOUTH BRENT

Scritch of metal over plate,
scrike of chair leg over slate.
Shrumph of air from open door,
scrunch of toast, then buttered more.

Chomp on bacon chunky-cooked,
a hurried meal, too lately booked.
Squelch of egg-yolk, sweetly spilled
on price of breakfast, quickly billed.

Devon voices, gravel growled
in burry rhythms, richly vowelled.
Swishing dish cloth swipes on wood,
clinking coins and thanks for food.

Stepping streetward, workshop bound.
Back to poets mulling sound
till silence sits, as words in head
are making music, metre led.

Susanne Smyth

CHANGES ROUND CHULEY ROAD, ASHBURTON TRADING ESTATE

Down St. Lawrence Lane the Methodists came,
and gave workshops in spirituality.
Along Blogishay Lane, software specialists came
to develop *Grey Matter's* acuity.

Near the empty rail station, a public ovation:
in drink at the *Silent Whistle*.
And when *Always Signs* shirked the *Old Umber Works*
moving to Pear Tree Cross,
A *Clipping Good Time* brought dog grooming sublime,
helping canines show who is the boss.

Then there's *Outdoor Experience* at pains to remind you
that indoors is all towed behind you.
Still, no fear of road fumes during outdoor ablutions,
next door is *Air Management Solutions*.

You can ride your horse hard till you find *Tuckers Yard*
and leave with a saw-horse of wood.
No more pollarding ash by the burn – no cut stash,
but *Pollards* will do your landscaping,
with piles of pike poles for pre-prepared holes
to finish a fence in the making.

Though attics have slats for the airing of wool,
Ashburton has slowly changed face:
no stamping in stannary, no longer with tannery,
now there's trade in the fields where wool-washing took place.

Susanne Smyth

8

MESH

The churn of tides and Teign
stirs up a clinker-build
of brig and saltern, lime and herring
streets divided, steam and diesel...
life stories bogged in overlap.

History hunter comes to fish:
names, dates, information.
Tale catcher, scale remover
threads inquisitive nets
among the town's foundations.

Passion of the seeker rakes the silt.
A long tongue of river speaks
of earth, fire, wind. And water
elemental in the sediment
of Sealeys, Hooks and Boynes.

Ian Royce Chamberlain

Sealey, Hook and Boynes are names of old fishing families in Teignmouth

NIGHT RIDE TO TEIGNMOUTH WITH KEATS

On top of the coach, wedged between the fabrics
of others and packages in wicker, leather and wood,
there is room only for breath, rain and the wind
that draws discomfort like a purse string.

I touch his arm, smell the damp in his greatcoat
through my fingertips. He'll never know. I am ghost.
I've clawed back time to see his skin in the night -
smooth and cold - stones in a streambed.

I hear the harsh compression of his lungs,
sense melancholy behind eyes that flicker.
His and all the other heads are bowed.
Those seats could be pews in a roofless church.

Inside, in the dry, a corpulent man smokes, reeks
of powder and porter. He rubs against a woman
clutching a bible that she'll not open,
even when the white sky of morning comes.

Opposite, a Wesleyan priest with a fixed scowl,
journeys with a younger man whose nose needs dabbing,
who may be a relative. They do not converse
but sometimes growl, like coach wheels riding stones.

All complain when those same wheels drop into ruts.
A wife across from the poet, sleepy in the rain,
tightens the grip on her child. Her husband
digs deeper into the scruff of a fresh dead hare.

Graham Burchell

GIBBET: BLACKDOWN HILL

Climbing uphill under a hot March sun
        grass crackles under our feet.
Ahead our shadows flow over rough ground

as if they would tow us along. Mine is bent,
        burdened.
This is not my shadow. It's a man's.

Sweaty heat, a long hard struggle
        with damp clothes sticking to us.
His last journey. I won't make it mine.

How has he come to this?
        Stealing a rabbit
to feed his wife and children

or has he taken a life?
        Our shadow pauses
is urged on.   Is he innocent?

I can't continue to the top.
        I call out to my friend
It's late. We must get back. It'll get dark.

We turn down to the village.
        My shadow uncurls,
walking upright beside me

but as light fades my shadow lengthens
        as though it still clung to the hill
and will not leave his side.

Jenny Hamlett

REPRIEVE

Something is sticking
to this fence post,
frogspawn.
I imagine the play-fight,
scooping it up
hurling handfuls, shrieking.

Inside the gelatinous mess
black dots hang, unmoving.
The last bored fling
of something disgusting
drips downwards,
blobs on leaves beneath.

I take my knife,
scrape it into a bag.
Here's a birthing-pool
under the trees,
sun-warmed
where blackbird forages,
elder spins concealment,
spawn melts into water.

I walk away - hear it still -
the hard thud,
the terrible interruption:
the song that was silenced
undrying, tide reversing,
into their bodies,
into each black space
the need to frog
surfacing.

Sue Proffitt

12

ANCESTRAL VOICES

Each night sleep loosens thought's mooring,
casts the mind adrift
in the warped cask of dreams
onto the stealthy flood of memory.
From the trees' mass owl calls
rise like smoke shapes from the dusk,
blow their spell in stillness
feathered with forgotten sounds
that drift from the abandoned caves,
stir light in strewn embers of the distant day.
They float us to the forest edge
where through its shifting screen
we glimpse fire blaze again, tools gleam,
mouths shape the syllables of speech,
move in command, or love.

Sometimes a ragged wind
buffets the mind's journey,
beats the torn sail in the face,
troubles with strange currents,
unexpected rocks, till,
coming back along the night dark lane
the eye is guided by a moving light,
the ear arrested by the hushed rush
of a swan's smooth flight
that, like a greeting from lost gods,
unfolds calm in turbulence,
carves a steady furrow
through imagination's wandering,
ploughs the swan-road
back to the ancestral hearth.

Helen Boyles

SOULIES BOTHY

Here, the cuckoo calls all night,
her voice magnified,
ricocheting against sheer sides of mountains.

I'm up early, wear no bra, don't wash,
pull a saucepan of water from the burn for tea.
Here, where earth and sky and loch meet

red-legged oyster catchers search the shore line for mussels.
In sandals I crunch the blue ovals of empty shells.
My boots are saturated.

I rub bog myrtle into my hands against midges,
stand close to the fallow deer with their white duster bottoms,
laugh as baby frogs jump on my bare toes.

Facilities are a long handled spade and mistakes are off limits.
I step gingerly over sphagnum moss
concealing nothing but water, mud and empty space.

We've had to walk in. We'll have to walk out.
Three days carrying tents, dried food, a medical kit.
Bridges are broken, rivers too deep to ford.

Here, the cuckoo's voice, louder than the siren of an ambulance
keeps me brilliantly awake
all through the Gaelic night's long dawn.

Jenny Hamlett

14

THE BAY AT THE BACK OF THE OCEAN, IONA
Camus Cuil an t-Saimh

I tumble down rabbity dunes
    delirious, to perfect white sand

this is my home
    my sou'westerly spray
        kelp-scrawled beaches
            milk-marbled waves

in Australia
    this northern skin burned
        my spirit limped
            longing for cool Atlantic breath

this scrawny wind
    blown five thousand miles
        thrums my skull
            washes me with shrill songs

the serpentine headland
    haloed in bright grey-green light
        tips into the caress
            the benediction of the west

Pat Fleming

UNDER EAST ANGLIAN SKIES

Warm Warm Warm
on feathers and fur
partridge and hare and on my
own downy skin.
We hide in the cornfield.

Warm warm under the blue bowl
of an East Anglian sky,
partridge and her brood,
hare in her hollow,
me lying on my back with
a book under my head.
Warm warm warm
the scent of the wheat rising
as it crackles, ready
for harvest. Small insects
tickling the backs of my legs.

Later, when the harvester
has been through and chased
away the partridge and the hare,
mashed up the nest and
flattened the hollow and
I have been given a wet sack
and a broom, fire watching,
I wait as the sky turns black.

Rosie Barrett

GIVING ME CHILLS

I stand by the edge of the woods
summer on Dartmoor
where the air keens
sharp with new wet grief
pulled south from the Arctic

where once frozen seas
now migrating whales and supertankers
follow new melt waters
where once frozen silence
bursts

I stand where the pounding wet
brought early blight to our potatoes
robbed us of pumpkins
laid our apple trees bare

will the long-eared bats catch enough
to lay down their white winter fat?

the pounding wet
washes everything
licks my face clean
mugs my voice
from me

Pat Fleming

*The amount of Arctic sea ice in summer has declined more than 40 percent since satellite
tracking began in the late 1970s, a trend that most scientists believe is primarily a
consequence of human activity. "It's hard even for people like me to believe, to see that
climate change is actually doing what our worst fears dictated," said a Rutgers University
scientist who studies the effect of sea ice on weather patterns. "It's starting to give me
chills, to tell you the truth."*

LITTORAL

Alone except for everything
I kneel and squint
this inch of beach
sniff listen
and induce the world

for instance
if I curl down my bottom lip
I can hold indefinitely
a tiny white quartz egg
against my chin
freeing my hands for marvels

or there's the wee
blue cornet shell
so minute I cannot have seen it
but I heard its notes
pleasantly baffling

which shows that the smallest things
can jump at you like tigers
and become horizons

take the little cowries
their gently incurled vulvas
protect unfathomable space
universes
where suns twirl
and there's always something
going supernova

Moira Lake

THREE CLAIMS FOR SUNSPOTS

1. Sunspots are fiercer than the moon.
2. They're holes which show the inside of the sun.
3. They shine as bright at midnight as they do at noon.

One of these facts was told by a buffoon;
let's check which statement needs to be undone.
Sunspots are fiercer than the moon:

True. If you could peel one, like a crotchet from a tune,
paste it into space, the moon *would* be outdone.
They shine as bright at midnight as they do at noon:

True. You can't see them, because the earth's balloon
has spun, but they give the light they've always done
and sunspots are fiercer than the moon.

They're holes which show the inside of the sun: You loon,
how can *holes* prelude flares, storms, a particle gun?
Still, they shine as bright at midnight as they do at noon.

So, to reiterate, we must impugn
the guy who claimed holes where there are none.
Remember, only: sunspots are fiercer than the moon
and shine as bright at midnight as they do at noon.

Simon Williams

QUARTZ – C$_{14}$

Luminescence gathered, stored and hoarded,
is safe while undisturbed;
dragged back up from the depths it fades
might not have been,
has lost its history
with its light.

I carbon date bright recollections
buried under strata of the years –
not lost, but surreptitiously
tested in the darkness,
held tight in deepest dreams.

Glimmers still escape:
the memory of a kiss,
your groan of longing and delight,
the look that lingered,
searching deeper, longer
boring down into the bedrock
of my being.

Exclude the present
obscure from sight,
or permanently lose the image as
it is exposed to light.

Alwyn Marriage

C$_{14}$ is a new method of carbon dating which relies on the fact that buried quartz retains luminescence from the last time it was exposed to the light. When it emerges from under ground, it loses its luminescence; but it can be tested first, to date quite accurately when was the last time it saw the light.

O BROOK

She loves it for the gasp in its name O
steep banks
       tumbles
   a constant wetness at its edges
like bleeds on cheap paper

she loves it for the islands it makes within itself
they could be organs heart lungs liver

she loves the high places it comes from
that it no longer smells of the hard men
that mined up there in rain and snow

she loves how it changes its tune
when she approaches
how it stops talking to itself
to tell her that it commiserates
then laughs because it is April
and even the rain when it comes
is fresh and green

she loves how two fritillaries
circle each other in a love tussle
while they cross to the far side settle
and drink lilac from the same thistle

Graham Burchell

AN INTERVAL

of shadows on the path,
the stillness of a garden before dawn,
the slow awakening
of uncertain voices drifting
on the wind
bird   human   real   imagined
faded to a whisper in long grass
or still to come.

The soft night rain clears away.

With a heavy grey beating of wings
a heron rises from the stream.

The sound of running water fills
the space below the blackbird's
early song and the calling of lambs.

Trees stretch out
against the growing light
their branches a message in semaphore
not yet to be read.

Bridget Thomasin

CORACIIFORMES

(kor – ah – see – form – eez)

thorn beak dashes
the corner of your eye
out of here out of here
green slip of a jig
splitting heartbeats
piercing facets of sunlight
into dressed diamonds
blue orchid grown up
from the branch
eyes all pupils
student of the masterclass
of fish

beating gravity to water
  water has prepared its shape
  water gives it free passage
sliding through a skin of oxygen
to the point
which is infant trout
breaking back to atmosphere
downstream
making for the dart
darting
between shafts
of white air

Simon Williams

CREEK HERON

A study in patience, elegant, deliberate,
on canvas wash of creek and sky,
furred edges blurred with the rain's breath,
a waiting heron scores the level greys
with his lean vertical.
Calm sentinel, he marks the axis
of the turning day, beak measuring
the shadow's angle on the sun's face,
anchors the shifting sky as light slants west.
Trawling the quiet of the afternoon,
sometimes he bends in scrupulous enquiry,
then shrugs to a question-mark
that punctuates the waiting space.
Purpose is poised in stillness
nerved to the rustle at the tide's edge
as broad feet flex and test the river bed
beneath its placid face,
thread the current's purl and flow,
translate its rhythms,
read the shadow flicker on the buried stone.
Then the mirror splinters with a quick stab
spearing movement;
the reflection wriggles, quivers,
shivers into fragments, thrashes in confusion
before the slivers coalesce to round the picture
which again hangs motionless, serene,
the eye alert above.

Helen Boyles

TROUTING

The pool was deep and dark as a coal seam; so cold it could stop your heart. I strained my eyes, saw only blackness, smelt only damp wood and moss. Stillness watched us warily. *It takes twenty minutes for nature to return to how it was before we interfered*, he said, so we sat on the bank

and waited

until birdsong stitched the silence; small rustlings re-awoke the undergrowth; an itch beetled blackly over my ankle. He threaded a red feathered fly on a hook, pulled his arm back, and with a slow flick, cast the line out across the pool

and we waited.

Think fish, he said. Lower yourself into the water; drink its dialect. Learn otter melt and heron shadow. Know when to stay deep, silted, and when to run with the urgency of egg weight. Mimic pebble fleck; shelter in the mouth of tree root; distinguish leaf from caterpillar fall. Only when you become fish will you know how to catch her, know which feathers tickle her, which colours entice. Even then, you must wait, as she waits, pulse slowing, blood cooling. You have to outsmart her and that takes time

so we waited

and when the late afternoon sun caramelised my skin, a wood pigeon's soft call floated out of the trees, settling over me like a soft felt hat. My eyelids gave in to gravity, and the warning I wanted to slip into the pool and let swim, slept in my throat.

Deep below, the brown trout stirred.

Fenella Montgomery

BALANCING ACT

Slowly we step across wide water   rock bulking, lichened and smooth
breathing: it's taken most of our life you shout and I can't look back
the river fizzing faster   water dark as Guinness

too late to turn back   what made us think we could risk it?
green rocks now, lank weed stranded   every stone a slippery stretch

the far bank receding   but this is what matters:
we are too far apart to clasp   alone together, balancing
on the far bank rowan berries shivering   poised to spill

Lyn Browne

AVON DAM

Pent up here, this weight of water,
this liquid muscle with its haul of life,
its microuniverse of microorganisms.

Held back here, this Samson strength,
this steamroller rollercoaster wave,
concealed beneath its innocent rippled skin.

One crack, one hole in this horseshoe battlement
and landscape would be changed forever,
brick and tile tossed aside, lives unmade

just as a word, a keepsake found can breach
my inner flood defence, or yours, let loose
a torrent dammed for years, primed to drown all

that tries to face it down,
leave a razed site, a zeroed ground.

Jennie Osborne

IT MAY BE THAT YOU WILL BECOME A RAILWAY SIDING

It may be that you will become a railway siding
somewhere on the way to nowhere,
shot past by main lines, their direction
and destination certain.

Your ballast may be overrun with ruderals,
your sleepers blurred with buddleia,
your red-white buffers a notion half-obscured.

It may be that you will become a depository
for old rolling stock – outmoded,
in need of repair which will never happen;

carriages will settle and rust,
dumb witness to the Doppler-fade
of passing trains, the sough of wind
in birch, the stonecrop's quiet creep.

At night there may be ugly shouts, graffiti,
the primal urge to injure what is already weak,
to shatter lichened windows, slash
sun-bleached upholstery...

> the late summer sun is a stillness
> pooled in you,
> the shiny black beetle a jewel on you,
> pale evening primrose your sentinel root,
> fireweed your strength
> and the length of your grasses and brambles
> a hush and a shush to small rodents
> and rabbits...

It may be that you will become a railway siding
somewhere on the way to nowhere.

Elizabeth Sutton

OUT OF THE WIND

...and it's like this he said, waving his arms, using his hands to
explain let's walk along the beach and I'll tell you...

So she held her shoes in her hand and listened.

It took from the steps, past the groins, under the pier
before the light began to break through
past the couple catching the last of summer
with the twins in Pampers
past two women crouching on concrete
almost to the end of the spit
where the tide covered the red sand

and as they walked
the dried kelp - golden - reminded him of her hair.

The space between people in September
gave them what they needed
by the time the beach ran out
they had covered their differences.

She dusted off her shoes
and with fresh feet they walked again on firm ground.

At last the sun shone and warmth seeped into their backs
as they disappeared up Morgan's Quay.

Susie Shelley

I REALLY TRIED TO LIKE TRAD JAZZ

scratchy old sounds lovingly transposed to cassette,
hundreds of them. Fats Waller,
Old Valley Stompers, The Hot Box Rag Band,
all written on spines in your peculiar scrawl.

Before we moved out to Knowle
you would drive me in the dirty white Capri
swishing swiftly down the A41
to my new primary school.

Enveloped in Player's Navy Cut fug,
Big Bertha would wail from the speaker at my knee.
Not speaking much, you were kind;
holding hands you walked me to playground's edge.

Much later, when I felt your solitude
I tried to reach you across the oestrogen sea;
confessed a liking for trad jazz.
You took me to a gig in Birmingham.

It was a smokin, stompin hollerin Hot Box;
wall-to-wall middle-aged men
drinking flat mild and warm Watney's;
chain-smoking, shouting over the din.

To be frank, it's not my music of choice,
but my way of connecting, of sharing love -
your fourth daughter out of five
being briefly No. 1.

Jackie Juno

LOUISE SINGS SOUL ON SUNDAYS

Louise sings soul on Sundays,
her notes seep under the door.
The lane is pooled with a false dawn
the robin is tricked into song.

The dogs pull dead things from gutters.
Snails creep up cracks in walls.
An old man scrapes a burnt plate,
his polished shoes wait in the hall.

Bats criss - cross the eaves of the Care Home,
its laundry hangs from a post.
A cat slips under a parked car
half scavenger, half ghost.

The kitchen boys share a joint
in the alley behind the pub.
A woman cries, rocking her belly,
on the edge of a chipped bathtub.

School girls drink vodka chasers,
hair washed in a cigarette haze,
as moonlight drops through the curtain
on Louise, singing soul,
on Sundays.

Helen Scadding

LOVE TRUCK

I was in love with a woman called Giraud.
She was my Aphrodite.
Then we fell out

It was like being run over
my guts squashed on love's highway
but I scooped them up
as we do.

Now I sometimes see Euro-trucks with
GIRAUD on the side in large letters
trundling their love-cargo all over the country

I say to myself
It's just another lorry
full of tomatoes and turnips

Giraud is like Smith or Brown
nothing special
nothing like Aphrodite

but when I see one roaring towards me
I hop out of the way like a frog
into the long grass of survival.

John Daniel

AUTUMN

It begins with a burst of purple on your tongue
staining teeth and lips with sweet anticipation of the glut
and only in the centre of the bush, deep among thorns
hang the juiciest, ripest fruit, each one fatter than the last
enticing you in.
Fingertips itch with prickle; wrists and ankles
tear with bramble scratch.

You play a game with yourself; can you reach that one
and that - even higher? As drunk as the gorging wasps
crawling over your hand, you want more.
The basket brims; your harvest begins to press on itself
and on the slow walk home, a puddle of purple oozes, drips
leaves a trail of your greed, dark as arterial blood
clotting on the dusty lane.

Fenella Montgomery

PRIMARY

Sunset bleeds through glass
floods my walls
I have known red so many ways

Thrill of forest fire
cloaked blades darkened sand
on bullfight afternoons
animal eyes bloodshot in the night
warning lights crimson scarlet

    scarlet
            Sylvia's dress

I have seen red too many times

When I go home
leave this granite prison
when they let me out
I will redecorate
repaint my life
ultramarine

Marion Cook

ROTHKO REDS (AT THE TATE GALLERY)

Transported by vast canvas sheets of reds:
each colour field of rubescence ignites
landscapes of fire-glow imagination.

This strange cathedral was spun from sugar.
These paintings serve as a rose window, whilst
disciples bathe in the blush of pigments.

Bubbling up from memory's studio
warming words, naming the old alchemies.
Litany recited as a rosary.

Cochineal, carmine and cinnabar,
crimson lake, corallin and paeonin,
fuchsin, magenta, madder, dragon's blood.

Cardinal works, wrought by this colour-smith:
woven layers of paint, blankets of dreams,
heat blood of devotees, who flush, inflamed.

Gillian Smith

HERB ROBERT

I get everywhere and am
a small piece of irrelevance

with my stripy flowers   tiny
            and   neat
and my careless   creeping
         creeping   habit
  I appear   optimistically

my casual mission
  to bring lightness to a structured world

I'm not out to cause trouble
  there's no
      depth to me
one gentle tug and
    up I come   roots and all

delicate even when I have grown
         e n o r m o u s

with tendrils shooting
                              out
         colonising whole walls
and borders
      and
dropping silently
             down onto
                    other walls
                         and borders
until scarlet lifelines
      rot away and each is
      on its own
cheerful   shallow   unthreatening
e v e r y w h e r e

Rosie Barrett

36

FESCUE *

This is
grass, how it grows,
how it blows in the wind,
sets seed, how it shimmers at the
curlew.

This is
architecture
in motion, sound waves, light,
nature's urge to curve, the wild world
bending.

This is
rustle, zither
at my fingertips, lip
music that is dry, friable,
fragile.

This is
small beauty, a
simple thing, wild-feathered,
not rare but dancing graceful in
the air.

This is
grass which bends and
does not break – but should we
imitate, bow down, or stand tall,
uncowed?

Shirley Wright

* *Je plie et ne romps pas (I bend and don't break) 'Le chêne et le roseau' – Fables de La Fontaine*

MEADOW

Movement catches;
a feather-flicker

tempts my feet from
razor-mown village green
to walk through tall grasses.
Crested dogstail, red fescue
shiver light, the merest edge,
merge waves of colour into heave and sway
parted by the wind to fold me
in seed and petal

where bees drink,
crane flies hover, soldier beetles
scurry over wild carrot, cornflower,
marigold, white clover, knapweed, teasel,

and the world turns,
all buzz and flurry.

Across the way
manicured borders marshal lawns
and distant slopes hang, monochrome,
ploughed like regiments of the innocent –
straight lines, sturdy structures
firm enough to bear a harvest
or a bier.

Here is borage, sainfoin, poppy,
yellow rattle, betony, scabious,
bold umbels of cow parsley,
hedgerows heady with dog rose;
and in the air the hum of purpose,
ache of abundance,
snow-dazzle of meadowsweet.

Shirley Wright

FEEDING THE BULLOCKS

I learned to low so
convincingly, the whole herd
came running, a stampede up-field
to line the barbed-wire fence.
That blank-eyed curiosity, press
of flank, shove and jostle
just to see me.
Beasts. Flick-flied, dung-deckled,
harrumphing.

I chucked windfall Bramleys
over the fence
for the jockeying hooves,
for the crush and slobber,
for the scent of friendship – cattle breath
and half-fermented apples.

Elizabeth Sutton

GATHERING

the fields are bolts of cloth

wrinkling with birds

until a stray thread is pulled

and half of the flock

folds itself over the other

to crease and quarter

new ground

while trees on the margin

are thick with their singing

till out of nowhere

the whump

of a thousand wings takes off

in one beat

not one stitch

touching another

a spindle of starlings

rise up in their thousands

a hank of black thread

drawn from the weave

Rebecca Gethin

AYLESBEARE COMMON

A gnarled and knobbly twig's a caterpillar,
a butterfly's one leaf among the green,
a feathered bunch of heather is a nightjar,
an adder is the shadow of a fern.
A poet's quit his job creating metaphors,
seeing how aptly life's evolved its own.

Mark Totterdell

SPINOSAURUS

The alpha-lizard, new beast on the block,
flexes its muscles, flashes vicious claws,
powers up the lethal chainsaw of its jaws,
and flaunts the sharp projections down its back.

Fleshed out from scattered scraps of bone turned stone,
restored to something very much like life,
across the widescreen landscape it galumphs,
pixelled in all the hottest dino-tones.

In prehistoric youth, I only knew
of Bronto, Steg, Triceratops, T. Rex,
constructing them from brittle plastic kits,
all monochromes, skewed limbs, the whiff of glue.

These latest days, I'm struggling to resolve
how we create, then recreate the past,
how we contrive to fill a void that vast,
how what's long dead continues to evolve.

Mark Totterdell

42

TO GRACE, BEING BORN BY THE THAMES

Dark portraits surround us, Grace,
weighty worthies watch us as we turn to face
a bright screen, where we tap and search
seeking your ancestor's sister:
lighthouse....shipwreck....rescue....

a winsome woman in bonnet forms,
her challenging eyes hold our gaze,
her half-smile blushed by sepia
fades into a solid jaw.
We print the Darling portrait as your present.

Waiting in the window of the
Gallery's penthouse tea-room,
we look out over roofs and river
toward your curled and unborn form
and dally in dilatory discussion.

Then over Whitehall's flapping flags,
over the Gallery's lead-leafed dome
a message moves in microwaves:
'Mother now in birth-room
but hours left to wait'.

We watch Big Ben, taking his time:
your father's family from the North,
your father, fretfully from the South;
while you and your Mama sleep
summoning strength for the big slide.

Three teas later, we elders rise:
up and down the river bank we go
making sympathetic magic, just as though
it is we who pass down the birth-canal
contracting to move toward the river's mouth.

Susanne Smyth

TWISTED SPIRE, ERMINGTON

Nearby is a church with a twist
in its spire – it turned to greet the beauty
of a local bride, and was frozen
in its tracks for the sin of desire.

So goes the myth.

Inside the church is the wooden pulpit
Violet carved, daughter of the vicar,
her ring of saints in wooden gowns,
their hands carved flat into their chests
or holding books or babies, or pointing
skywards,

all but one, who stretches out his hands
in walnut sleeves, inviting you to hold them
in yours, and when you do,
you can feel how the wood has smoothed to a polish
and the fingers have been stroked to a blur,
still warm as if they have danced around a maypole
on a hot village afternoon, or been circled
in the palm of a parish child longing to grow up.

So stories go, leaping from wood to stone to flesh.

Jane Spiro

SAMPLER CIRCA 1918

A length of fine cotton folded twice to shape an envelope.
White thread on white, cross and backstitched.
The makings of a nightgown case, fashioned
by my grandfather during convalescence.

When he came back, damaged beyond the call of duty,
I'm told *they learned him to embroider* –
satin, stem and chain,
to count and draw the threads of cutwork,
stitch by hand regular as any machine,
blind hem, run and fell.

Hilary Jupp

CRACKING WALNUTS

I sat low
At a linen table
Watching
Your long soft palm
Squeezing two walnuts.
Rolling them together.
A hard hollow scrape.
Pressing fleshy mounts
Into the gnarl.

I could not look at you.
Frightened of seeing pain.
Only saw knuckles tighten
With this gasp of strength
That came from another life.
I held my own breath
As your press groaned,
Cracking a cranium
Against its own wall.

A quiet implosion and release.
You opened a rhubarb hand,
Full of dust and nut oil,
Peppered with shard.
Held it still, for me
To pick small, sweet pieces
With fingertips relieved
To touch the hand
That was mine again.

Helen Scadding

BERNARD

My dark-eyed uncle
a young man of untroubled beauty,
prodigal son, unknown, with crinkly hair
lies in a tin box

in a wallet made of red and black leather
from Cameroon, where he was sent off to work
as a last resort by a family
who had run out of ideas, I think.

There is a crystal-paper pocket
stuffed with photos of white men
in white socks and colonial hats,
posing contentedly with black beauties
at the market in the 50s

and Bernard, who smokes and always smiles,
a smile as wide as the span of my hand
is holding his black woman by the waist
by the arm, the same woman, held.

Bernard, not that tall, fell like a tree at 26.

'But what did he die of?' I asked, a child
intrigued by this modern-day Rimbaud
caught by the only photo in my parents' bedroom.

'He caught malaria in a river and died'
Liars! He was poisoned by a jealous local,
lost his love and life to a rival lover
and my father lost his favourite brother.

Fifty years on, his photo stares at me.
He tries to tell me something, smiling so clearly
but it's nothing like the feeling that everything is right,
the feeling that you get in black and white photographs.

Mélisande Fitzsimons

THE ANDERSON SHELTER

They bunkered down close by a granite wall outcropped with oaks.
Bombed out of their two up-two down,
where belongings ironed neat as pins
had crammed alcoves and ottomans;
a family: two adults, seven kids and a dog
made home in an arc of corrugated iron.

Given a blanket of cloud they slept like sardines in a tin,
angled in under a spread of coats.
Exposed to stars they shuddered with the ground.
Beyond the copse the pitch of sky blooded raw.
Above, on the plateau of the moor,
anti-aircraft guns clattered through the night.

With hands together eyes closed tight, they prayed to hear
the water in a nearby trough trickle with morning light

Hilary Jupp

STATE OF EMERGENCY
In memory of Annette McGavigan d. 1971

Below the city's walls on the Bogside
the flats stand in squadrons - numbered, uniform,
their walls pebble-dash thin. Faces at windows

witness what's going on at the barricades.
Next door's TV is turned up against the noise
of trouble outside. A girl in white socks

slams the front door behind her as she runs to the shop.
On her way back she sees friends in the crowds
watching the youths keeping the soldiers at bay.

It's the usual stuff so she slips off home:
Dad will complain if his chips aren't hot.
A gun goes off, more firing follows ...

Glass shatters, then screams, footsteps running.
The screams don't stop. Behind the line –
radio gabble, intakes of breath.

The squaddies raise their sights. That burning
in the back of your throat ...
is the stench of war breaking out in the streets.

Rebecca Gethin

*Annette McGavigan was 14 years old and lived in Drumcliff Avenue, Derry. She was shot in
the back of the head by a British soldier on September 6th 1971. A mural of her in Derry is a
reminder of the need for peace.*

TWO SISTERS

are dying.

The one who loves her garden must go North.
It is dark, too cold for her fingers in the earth.
Splinters cut her hands, scraping the soil's hard edge.
In the black rocks there are seams of green
but the sun's lemon-wedge light is short;
she must pull herself in at dusk.

The one who hates her garden must go West,
where the earth turns all night under a gold sky.
There is no sunrise here in this fallow silence,
just the stirring of sleepless worms
where she keeps company with other kneelers,
hands rising and falling like sickles over the soil.

That's how it is.

Sue Proffitt

ONCE BESIDE A TIME

At the pool with its sludge-tracked
changing rooms and clammy air
smelling of people no longer there,
someone's goggles hang from a hook.

I squeeze myself into a black number,
make like I'm dancing and turn
to find my own ghost with my children,
a hundred echoing visits – undressing,
scrambling clothes into lockers.
Don't run. Don't slip.

I am in no hurry.
I slide in at no beat, pointed as a knife,
till I am green shimmer
and way over my head.

Rose Cook

WOODWORK

The woodwork master, Mr Beech –
that was his name, he is not fictitious –
ran a workshop full of salad forks

and spoons. The roughs had prongs
and dimples from the start. We learned
much about sandpaper; how it's graded.

'Graded grains make smoother spoons',
said Mr Beech. In the second year, we
made lamps in the shape of sailing boats,

where the translucent shades were the sails.
We shaped the prows with a band saw;
I cut the point off mine, by accident.

'No, you can't have another blank', said Mr Beech,
'Wood doesn't grow on trees, you know'.

Simon Williams

TRACES

Searching for the lost,
the absent, the unnamed

a trace remains,
something left behind

where frost under grey skies
cracks open the idea of childhood

rich with hidden places
waiting to be found.

What we have never known
brings us here

where once I told you
the beginning was rain.

Bridget Thomasin

BLUE, YELLOW, RED, BLACK

He brings me a gift.
He places it carefully among the ornaments:
so much more beautiful,
so much more caught, lying there,
blue and yellow harmonics, visionary
blue and yellow, tendered in the detail,
bloody art and artlessness,
blood-heat.. feathered... fascinator...

among yards of cheap red tinsel,
among a hoard of tawdry trinkets,
never able to pull them from the nesting box,
never able to hang them on the tree, cut down
for solstice, without the sting of this
for solstice, when night is at its darkness:
blue tit, unblemished still in death,
black cat, with no knowledge of his gift.

Susan Taylor

EPIPHANY AT PENNANCE FARM

A metal-grey light flows from the Arctic
      hail snow frost.

I climb slowly, feet too cold to feel
      stones through my boots

      past a brown pond
past black-plastic barrels of hay stacked to cloud height.

A voice calls out from the barn.

I thread my way past machinery and sacks.
      Megan, in her working clothes
is surrounded by sheep

      bunched together in the black straw
their faces framed by grey wool clouds.
She tells me the ones with curly hair are her own.

Do you lamb them? She smiles. *Of course she does.*
At night? How do you cope with college?

She shrugs.
      She's a farmer's daughter and that's the way it is.

I remember dragging hay on sledges through deep snow
      feeding the ponies after school
heaving water, humping tack

oiling hooves, untangling tails,
      pulling up ragwort from the field
the wet sweaty stink of horse.

New life out of old dark stays with me when I leave,
      a kick in my stride as I walk
the metallic clouds glistening.

Jenny Hamlett

SNOW WORK

The snow has grounded the workers
and only snow-work snow-play
is to be done today.

The neighbour has ditched his dawn start
and instead shovels the white dune of his
doorstep into a dump on the open drive,
builds it load by load into a lolling
giant anthill half his height.

Now he squats before the ghost
he has made, his mittened paws patting
and shaping, freeing soft flakes of quartz
onto his damp sleeve, summoning the white
space into form with his hands,

then stands, complete, to view his work,
a smiling moon face with pudding cheeks,
pool-pebble eyes and deep drawn grin,
bundled warm inside a loosely knotted scarf,
plump and rooted to his ground.

Another kind of work was done today,
another kind of getting-things-done,
built like the seasons, to come and go,
built because the moment told you so.

Jane Spiro

CONSIDERING JANUARY

The way the mercury creeps down, then drops
still further through the huddled hours of sleep.
The way the snow falls, silent, lethal, soft,
forms strange impressions, takes prints from passing fox.
How light comes late, how world is dumb, bleak, white.
The way that air is ice and ground is lead,
wind sears the face, gnaws at the hands, numbs feet.
See how the trees preach monochrome.

The way the globe tilts back towards the sun,
how heads are lifted at the harsh high call
of migrant geese skeining across the sky.
How snowdrop leaves spear upward through the earth,
the first flower pendulous and pure.
The way the bud was there before you knew.

Elizabeth Sutton

OBSCURED

Driving across the moor, from dark to light,
light to dark, the clouds toy with me,
hang up curtains, take them down, steal the road,
cause trees to swoon, trespass into night.

Blinding hail next, and then ponies in my way –
March: my friend spoke to me so confidently
in those last weeks, last year – the view's obscured again
by ribbons of sleet, winter's protracted stay.

I argue with it, as I drive. Nearly April, nearly a year,
as sun filches through, sneaking up behind me
as that month snuck up on her. I'm skidding down a hill now,
all bets off, though she'd insisted the weather would clear.

Now it's to do with shadows, sticking to the road ahead,
championing the direct route, as gradually, I descend.

Julie-Ann Rowell

HERON CHICK

We kept the shell to remember,
like holding on to a melody
when the song is lost.

Can we be certain we really saw
that sweep at dusk,
the grace of circles
traced in fading light?

Lyn Browne

NATURAL SELECTION
i.m. Nigel Cameron, artist, fellow Moor Poet

We live with the whispering flight plans of birds.
Sometimes, when swallows skim the lanes,
we walk tall above them.

In July we chance on flashy colonies of butterflies
in dolly mixture etymology.

Thrushes fly in and out of kitchens
and where there's a plate glass door that's closed,
they could break their necks against it.

A wise old poet I knew cut out the shape of a hawk
and stuck it on his studio glass –
that stopped them.

In this soft-aired landscape, we moor poets
are drawn to beat the bounds, gather wool strands,
moonbathe, dream of sheep.

Susan Taylor